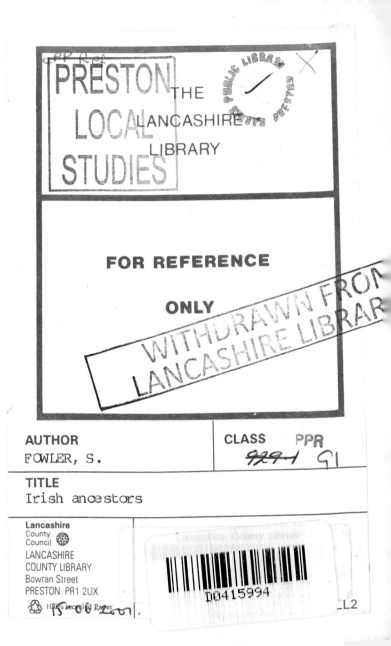

Public Record Office
Pocket Guides to Family History

TRACING

IRISH ANCESTORS

Simon Fowler

PUBLIC RECORD OFFICE

Public Record Office
Richmond
Surrey
TW9 4DU

ISBN 1 903365 03 1

A catalogue card for this book
is available from the British Library

084230022

PPR

Front cover: two girls, County Donegal
Photograph by Robert Banks of Manchester
Registered by him for copyright 4 May 1889
(COPY 1/369)

Printed by Cromwell Press, Trowbridge, Wiltshire

CONTENTS

INTRODUCTION

It has recently been estimated that over 70 million people around the world can claim descent from Irish men and women. An increasing number of them are researching their ancestors, and as a result more and more finding aids, databases and websites are being developed to help family historians. Tracing Irish ancestors can be trickier than finding English or Scottish forebears. Firstly, until the beginning of the nineteenth century it was unusual for Catholics to appear in the records. Since there was active discrimination against Catholicism, there are few parish registers for Catholic churches. And as most people were desperately poor, they rarely left wills or records of property transactions.

Secondly, fire destroyed the holdings of the Public Record Office of Ireland (the predecessor of the National Archives) at the Four Courts in Dublin in 1922. The losses included most Church of Ireland parish registers and considerable numbers of pre-1857 wills. Spirited attempts have been made to re-create these collections, but inevitably much has been lost that can never be recovered.

A third problem is that, if your ancestors emigrated, it can be very difficult to identify which part of Ireland they came from, particularly if they went to mainland Britain. However, considerable efforts have been made to publish lists of passengers arriving in North America and elsewhere, so this problem may not be insurmountable.

Despite these problems, researchers do succeed in tracing their Irish ancestors. With a bit of luck and perseverance, there is no reason why you should not join them.

Before you start your research, it is important to understand a bit about the political geography of the island of Ireland. Until 1922 Ireland was part of the United Kingdom; in 1922 the Irish Free State (now the Republic of Ireland) was created. The mainly Protestant six counties of Northern Ireland, however, remained part of the UK. If your ancestor came from the North, you will probably need to visit Belfast, although some duplicate material can be found at the National Archives and other centres in Dublin. However, if your ancestor came from the South, most are in Dublin. There is also a network of county heritage centres, in both the North and South, which may prove useful.

This Pocket Guide covers material held by the Public Record Office (PRO) at Kew. In theory, at least, these records relate mainly to the British administration of Ireland before 1922; but in fact there is considerably more than this of value to the family historian. The Family Records Centre (FRC) in London is also an important resource, because it has material about Irish people who lived in England.

In addition, the Guide offers an introduction to major sources in Ireland (both North and South). The most important resources are the National Archives of Ireland in Dublin; the Public Record Office of Northern Ireland (PRONI); and the General Register Offices (GRO) in Dublin and Belfast. A considerable amount of genealogical material is also held in the library of the Society of Genealogists (SoG) in London. The Family History Centres of the Church of Jesus Christ of Latter-day Saints (LDS), which are scattered throughout Britain, have microfilm of some of these records.

HISTORICAL BACKGROUND

Irelands's relations with England

During the medieval period, English kings mounted a number of campaigns to pacify the Celtic chieftains. By 1603 they had largely been successful. After the Reformation, when England became Protestant but the Irish remained Catholic, a religious element entered into the conflict and Catholicism was suppressed. In 1690 William III defeated James II's forces at the Battle of the Boyne, thus ensuring English dominance of Ireland.

During the first half of the seventeenth century Protestant settlers from England and Scotland arrived in Ulster (roughly the area occupied by Northern Ireland today). These 'plantations', as they were known, were given land taken from long-standing Catholic landowners. Initially these new communities, and particularly their leaders, had considerable sympathy towards aspirations for self-government for Ireland. This changed during the nineteenth century into implacable opposition and a passionate desire to maintain the union with Britain – hence the fact that these communities came to be known as 'Unionists'.

Until 1801 Ireland had a measure of self-government and its own Parliament. In 1800, following the defeat of the rebellion of United Irishmen (Catholic and Protestant), the Irish Parliament passed the Act of Union. Between 1801, when the Act came into force, and 1918, a hundred Irish MPs sat in Parliament in London. Local administration was now vested in the Viceroy, a politician who usually sat in the British cabinet. It was always an uneasy union. The British remained largely insensitive to the needs of the Irish people: Catholicism, the faith of the majority, remained illegal until 1830 (although there was considerable toleration from the late 1770s). The famines of the 1840s left bitter memories among those who were forced to emigrate, as well as those who remained behind. Economically, Ireland remained undeveloped. In the main, Irish industry and agriculture could not compete with their Scottish and English rivals.

During the nineteenth century a succession of nationalist politicians, most famously Daniel O'Connell and Charles Stuart Parnell, sought to draw attention to Ireland's plight and argued for self-rule. Irish matters were an important factor in British politics throughout the nineteenth century. In the 30 years or so before 1914 there was controversy over the issues of land reform and the amount of devolution (or Home Rule, as it was known) that should be granted.

The catalyst for Irish independence came during the First World War, beginning with the failed Easter Rising of 1916. The situation was inflamed by insensitive policing by British forces, and a state of rebellion and guerrilla warfare resulted. A treaty offering dominion status to Ireland, and thus creating the Irish Free State, was agreed in 1921, although arguments over whether to accept the oath of allegiance to the crown, as laid down in the treaty, led to a bitter civil war in 1922. The new Free State became the Republic of Ireland in 1949, on leaving the Commonwealth.

The mainly Protestant area in the north-east of the island, however, was opposed to Home Rule (or rather rule by the Catholic majority). In 1920 the six counties of Antrim – Armagh, Down, Fermanagh, Londonderry and Tyrone – became the Province of Northern Ireland within the United

Kingdom. Here the Catholic minority remained very much second-class citizens, a fact which fuelled 'the Troubles' that began in 1969. At the time of writing the most significant subsequent peace deal, the Good Friday agreement of 1999, is in the process of being implemented.

Migration

There has been migration from Ireland for many hundreds of years. Most Irish people choosing to leave have done so for economic reasons, and have gone to Britain, America or Australia.

Irish people began to arrive in England during medieval times, and often found seasonal work on farms and market gardens. During the nineteenth century demand for labour in the new factories of the Industrial Revolution began to attract migrants from Ireland. The census of 1841 identified 400,000 Irish-born people in London.

From the seventeenth century, Irish people also began to go to the new colonies in America. Many of them were from the Protestant Scots–Irish settlements in Ulster, and did much to explore and open up the western frontier along the Appalachian Mountains.

Catholic emigration to America really began in the 1820s. Between 1820 and 1930, 4.5 million Irish people went to the United States. Perhaps another 500,000 went to Canada (many of whom eventually ended up in the States), and 350,000 to Australia and New Zealand. No figure exists for migration to Britain, but in 1861 census enumerators found that 600,000 people had been born in Ireland.

The catalyst for this emigration was the poverty of rural Ireland. In particular, the Great Famine, between 1845 and 1849, forced 2 million people to emigrate – about a quarter of the population of the island. In 1841, the population of Ireland was over 8 million, but by 1901 this had declined to just 4.5 million, making Ireland the only country in Europe whose population fell during the century. The flight from Ireland continued in the twentieth century. As late as 1969, it was estimated that there were 750,000 Irish migrants in Britain.

In Britain, the favourite destinations of Irish migrants were London and Liverpool and other Lancashire towns. In 1851, 22 per cent of Liverpool's population and 13 per cent of Manchester's was Irish-born. Migrants from the north of Ireland tended to go to the lowlands of Scotland. About 1,000 emigrants a week were arriving in Glasgow during 1848.

The Irish were poor, unskilled and uneducated, and often had only a rudimentary grasp of English. They also faced hostility and discrimination from the native-born population. They settled together, usually in the poorest districts of a town, and undertook the most menial work. The 1881 census revealed that 82 per cent of Irish-born men were day-labourers, particularly in the building trades.

Over the past decade, however, this pattern of emigration seems to have come to an end. The growth of the Irish economy has meant that Ireland has seen a net influx of population for the first time in centuries.

RESEARCHING IRISH ANCESTORS IN ENGLAND

The Public Record Office

The Public Record Office is the national archive of the United Kingdom – and England and Wales. The PRO has records created or acquired by the central government in Whitehall and the central law courts over more than 900 years. As explained above, the Republic of Ireland and Northern Ireland have their own national archives in Dublin and Belfast respectively, which have records of purely Irish interest. As a result, the PRO is not the first place to visit when searching for Irish ancestors. That said, there is material about many Irish men (and a few women) at the PRO. For a guide to family history records at the PRO, see Bevan, *Tracing Your Ancestors*.

▶ **Public Record Office**
  Kew
  Richmond
  Surrey TW9 4DU
  General telephone: 020 8876 3444
  Telephone number for enquiries: 020 8392 5200
  Internet: http://www.pro.gov.uk/

Opening times (closed Sundays and Bank Holidays):

Monday	9 a.m. to 5 p.m.
Tuesday	10 a.m. to 7 p.m.
Wednesday	9 a.m. to 5 p.m.
Thursday	9 a.m. to 7 p.m.
Friday	9 a.m. to 5 p.m.
Saturday	9.30 a.m. to 5 p.m.

No appointment is needed to visit the PRO in Kew, but you will need a reader's ticket to gain access to the research areas. To obtain a ticket, you need to take with you a full UK driving licence or a UK banker's card or a passport if you are a British citizen; and your passport or national identity card if you are not. Note that the last time for ordering documents is 4 p.m. on Mondays, Wednesdays and Fridays; 4.30 p.m. on Tuesdays and Thursdays, and 2.30 p.m. on Saturdays.

What to take with you to the PRO

- £1 coin (refundable) so you can leave any baggage in a locker

- money or a credit card if you are intending to buy copies of any records

- pencil (ink and rubbers are not allowed at Kew in case they damage original records, but they are allowed at the FRC)

- paper to record what you find (notebooks are allowed at both the FRC and Kew, but at Kew no more than six loose sheets are permitted)

- a record of any research you have done so far, to make sure you don't go through anything twice, unnecessarily

- a laptop computer, if you wish

Records at the PRO are normally kept together according to the government department that created them. Departments are given prefixes that help you identify them. The War

Office, for example, is WO and the Foreign Office is FO. Within each department, similar types of records form separate series. Each of these series is assigned a unique number. Thus, the series WO 95, for example, contains war diaries of the First World War; WO 96, militia attestation papers; and WO 97, soldiers' documents between 1760 and 1913. Within each series, each piece – normally a file or volume – is given a unique reference. It is this three-part reference that you order, and need to quote in correspondence or in any book.

For most popular family history searches at the PRO, simple explanatory leaflets are available to guide you to your reference. To make a search not covered by these leaflets, you will need to use the PRO's catalogue, which is available both on paper and electronically. The electronic catalogue can be searched by subject. It is now easy to find, for example, the 95 references to the Connaught Rangers by typing their name into the computer. The electronic catalogue is also available through the PRO's website. The paper and electronic versions of the catalogue are available at Kew.

Records relating to Ireland and the Irish can be found in many places. There are some 337 series of records and 28,000 individual pieces alone that have Ireland or Irish in the title, although it has to be said that relatively few of these entries are likely to be of immediate use to family historians. On the other hand, there are many records not specifically labelled as 'Irish' that contain material of interest to researchers tracing ancestors from across the water. There is a useful PRO leaflet entitled *Irish Genealogy* (Overseas Records Information 9), which offers some suggestions, particularly on tackling the printed and older material. The leaflet can be downloaded from the PRO's website (http://www.pro.gov.uk).

Military records

The British Army, in particular, was popular with many young Irish men who wanted to escape the grinding poverty of home. In the middle of the nineteenth century Irishmen made up a substantial proportion of other ranks (ordinary soldiers). In addition, a considerable proportion of officers came from Anglo-Irish families.

The Public Record Office has records for men and women who left the services before the end of 1920. Whether you are looking for the records of a serviceman or an officer, it can help if you know roughly when he was in the forces, and the regiment, ship or unit he served with.

There were, and still are, a number of specifically Irish regiments. They were treated in exactly the same way as their English, Welsh or Scottish counterparts. It was customary before the First World War for regiments to recruit primarily within a local district, but this did not prevent Irish men from joining English regiments.

It is important to recognize the difference between officers, non-commissioned officers (NCOs) and other ranks (ratings in the Navy). NCOs and ordinary soldiers, sailors and airmen made up the vast majority of the armed forces. Their records will be found in different series from those of officers. Officers are also listed in published *Army Lists*, *Navy Lists*, and *Air Force Lists*, and it is often possible to trace the outline of their careers from these publications. Service records vary greatly in format, but they all contain roughly the same information.

The General Register Office (GRO) in Dublin has some records relating to Irish service personnel. These include records of deaths in the First World War, and returns of births, marriages and deaths of Irish persons at military stations abroad between 1881 and 1921. Similar material for Northern Ireland from 1930 is at the General Register Office (GRO) in Belfast.

Army – Officers

From 1740, all officers were listed in the published *Army List*, which appeared at least annually. If your ancestor is not in the *List*, then he was not an officer. There was a private rival publication between 1839 and 1915 – *Hart's Army List* – which contains a certain amount of biographical information, particularly about the campaigns that officers served in. Both series can be consulted at Kew.

For the nineteenth century, there are several different series of records detailing the service of officers. Fortunately, the PRO holds an alphabetical card index to these records.

All officers receive a royal commission. The PRO has correspondence about the purchase and sale of commissions between 1793 and 1871, in series WO 31. This contains a great deal of valuable genealogical material. Records of military commissions and appointments of Irish officers between 1768 and 1877 are in HO 123.

Before 1871, officers went on half-pay when they retired – that is, they were paid a pension although they were, in theory at least, ready to be called up at any time. Retired officers continued to be listed in the *Army Lists*. There are registers and correspondence about the payment of pensions up to 1921, including some records for pensions paid to widows and children.

Service records for the First World War are now available at the PRO. About 85 per cent survive, but they can be disappointing because they are often just about pension claims.

Army – Other ranks

Before the 1880s, it is very helpful to know the regiment that the soldier served with. This can be difficult to discover. It may sometimes be possible to identify it from buttons or insignia on uniforms in old photographs. Alternatively, a man may simply have joined the regiment stationed near to where he lived. Records of the effects of dead soldiers are arranged alphabetically and these may help identify a regiment.

The most useful records are the soldiers' documents, in series WO 97, which are service records for men who received a pension between 1760 and 1913. There are few records before 1790. Before 1883 they are arranged by regiment. However, the Friends of the PRO have indexed the soldiers' documents up to 1854 by surname, and this index is available at the PRO. The documents indicate when and where a man served, promotions, disciplinary offences, place of and age on enlistment, and reason for discharge. They also often list wives and children. Similar documents for Irish men who were discharged between 1783 and 1822 are in WO 119.

Up to two-thirds of the Army service records for the period between 1914 and the end of 1920 were destroyed in the Second World War. Those documents that survived are in series WO 363 and are in the process of being microfilmed in surname order. The project should be completed by 30 April 2002. In the meantime, the enquiry helpline on 020 8392 5200 will tell you which surnames have been filmed.

These records contain information about the place and date of enlistment, medical details, disciplinary record and other details, although what is in each document varies greatly. There is also a series of service records, in WO 364, for men who received a pension after the First World War (for long service or medical discharge). What these records don't tell you much about is the experience of the man at the front. For this, you will need to consult the battalion war diaries in WO 95 (although these do not usually mention individuals by name).

An alternative source is the muster rolls, which listed all the men in a regiment (including officers) and were compiled monthly. They indicate a man's pay, offences committed during the previous month, and the location of the regiment. They begin in 1732 and end in 1898.

Men who had served the full period of enlistment or been wounded while serving were entitled to a pension from the Royal Kilmainham Hospital, the Irish equivalent of the Royal Chelsea Hospital. There are a variety of different records to help. Most men were out-pensioners – that is, they received a pension at home – rather than in-pensioners, who lived in the hospital itself. Admission registers for both in-pensions and out-pensions between 1794 and 1922 are in WO 118. This series also includes lists of in-pensioners. Kilmainham was closed in 1928, when the work of the Hospital and many of the in-pensioners were transferred to Chelsea.

Officers and men also appear on campaign medal rolls, which before 1913 are in WO 100. During the First World War almost all men who served in the Army were entitled to at least two campaign medals. The medal record cards at the PRO will tell you which regiment(s) a man served with, which medals he was entitled to, and approximately when and where he served.

Militia records

Militia muster rolls between 1793 and 1876 are in WO 13. In the same series are musters of volunteers, 1797–1814 and 1873–8. They are arranged by county and list alphabetically men's names, their ages and parish.

For more information about Army service records, see the PRO Pocket Guide *Using Army Records* or S. Fowler and W. Spencer, *Army Service Records for Family Historians*.

Royal Air Force and Royal Navy

Neither the Royal Air Force nor the Royal Navy differentiated recruits from Ireland in any way.

For the RAF, the service records generally cover those who served in the First World War. Records for those who served after 1919 (airmen and women) and the mid-1920s (officers) are still with the Ministry of Defence. Records of officers are in AIR 76, and other ranks in AIR 79.

Records for the Navy can be difficult to use. There are no service records for ratings until 1853. Men were discharged at the end of each voyage, so there was no continuity of service. You need to know the names of the ships an individual served with, and these may include time in the merchant navy. The only really useful sources are ships' muster books and, to a lesser extent, logbooks.

In 1853 continuous service engagement books were introduced, and these formed the basis of service records until 1923. The information contained in these registers is by no means as full as their Army equivalents, but you should be able to find dates of entry and discharge, ships served on, promotions, disciplinary records and some personal details. These records are in series ADM 139 and ADM 188.

Officers' service records are in some ways similar to their Army equivalents. All naval officers are listed in the *Navy List*, published at least annually. Service registers are in series ADM 196 and most entries are in the period between 1840 and 1920 – although there are some retrospective entries back as far as 1756, and deaths up to 1966 are also noted. These records will give you the ships served on, promotions, some personal details, and the name of any spouse.

Medal rolls for both gallantry and campaign medals are in ADM 171. They include awards for the First World War. Ships' logbooks are another useful source, although they rarely mention individuals. They are in ADM 53.

Royal Marines

The Royal Marines' service records are fairly easy to use, although you will need to know which division a man served with (that is, Chatham, Plymouth, Portsmouth or Woolwich). Service records for other ranks between 1759 and 1920 are in ADM 159. Officers' service records are exactly the same as for their Naval counterparts.

Further reading

For the RAF, see W. Spencer, *Air Force Records for Family Historians* (PRO, 2000). For the Royal Navy, see the PRO Pocket Guide *Using Navy Records* (PRO, 2000); and for the Royal Marines, see G. Thomas, *Records of the Royal Marines* (PRO, 1995).

The fallen of two world wars

The Commonwealth War Graves Commission was set up to commemorate the dead of the First World War and has done its best to find and record as many war deaths of British and Commonwealth men as possible from 1914 to the present. It is perhaps best known for the hundreds of carefully tended cemeteries scattered through northern France and Belgium. Its database is now online at http://www.cwgc.org and will tell you where a man is buried, when he died and the unit he served with. You can also write to the Commonwealth War Graves Commission, 2 Marlow Road, Maidenhead, SL6 7DX or ring on 01628 34221.

For the First World War, most of the officers and other ranks are recorded in *Soldiers Died in the Great War*. Originally this was a multi-volume book, but it has recently been put onto CD-ROM, which makes it very easy to search. The information contained about individuals varies and is not always accurate, but it will indicate where a man died, his rank and the regiment he was with. It may also tell you where and when a man enlisted and his age at enlistment. Copies can be used at the PRO and at the library of the Society of Genealogists.

Because of fears over Irish loyalty during the First World War, conscription was never introduced in Northern Ireland. Even so, many tens of thousands of Irish men from both north and south volunteered for service. Some 35,000 lost their lives between 1914 and 1918 and are commemorated in the same way as their British comrades. A memorial to their memory exists in Dublin, and an Island of Ireland Peace Park commemorating soldiers from both parts of Ireland was opened in 1998 at Messines near Ypres. All Irish soldiers who died in the First World War are listed in *Ireland's Memorial Records, 1914–1918* (1923), which can be found at the Society of Genealogists. Each entry in the book contains the place of birth, date of death, regiment served in and regimental number.

During the Second World War, again, there was no conscription in Northern Ireland. Although the Irish Free State was neutral, many men from all over Ireland joined the British armed forces. There is a roll of honour for men who died in the Second World War at the PRO in record series WO 304, which includes Irish citizens. This too is now available on CD-ROM. Copies can be used in the PRO and SoG libraries. The GRO in Belfast has records of the deaths of people born in Northern Ireland who died on war service between 1939 and 1948.

Merchant seamen

Records of merchant seamen and shipping can be tricky to use, partly because the survival of records tends to be patchy, but mainly because there was no central registry of merchant seamen until 1913, apart from the period between 1835 and 1857. As a result, you will probably need to search a variety of series.

The Merchant Shipping Act of 1835 ordered the registration of merchant seamen. Registers of seamen, and associated indexes, were kept between 1835 and 1857 and are now in series BT 112, BT 119 and BT 120. In addition, there are registers in BT 113 containing applications for seamen's tickets between 1845 and 1853. All these registers contain some personal details, such as age and place of birth, and indicate which ships a man served on.

The central registry was abandoned in 1857. It was not until 1913 that a new Central Index Register was established. This lasted until 1941, although many of the records for the period 1913–20 have been destroyed. Index cards for individuals, which include photographs as well as the usual personal details, are on microfiche at the PRO in series BT 348–350 and BT 364.

There are certificates of competency for masters and mates of ships, 1845–1921 (BT 122–BT 127); engineers, 1862–1921 (BT 139–142); and skippers and mates of fishing boats, 1883–1930 (BT 129, BT 130, BT 138). After 1910 a combined index was started (BT 352). These index cards cover the period up to 1930 (although there are some entries beyond this date) and give name, place and year of birth, date and place of issue of certificate, and rank examined. Deaths, injuries and retirement are often mentioned in these records. Applications for certificates up to 1928 are at the National Maritime Museum. After this, the system changed and there are no equivalent documents.

From 1747, ships were supposed to maintain lists of personnel on board. However, few of these musters survive before 1835, when they were replaced by agreements and crew lists. Masters of ships of more than 80 tons had to enter into a written agreement with each crew member about conditions of service. Copies had to be sent to the Registrar General of Shipping and Seamen, together with lists of crew members (which include some personal details) and often, from 1850, ships' logs. Between 1835 and 1857 these records are in BT 98. After 1857 they can be found in series BT 99, BT 144 and BT 165. However, after 1861 the PRO has only a 10 per cent sample. The remaining crew lists are at either the National Maritime Museum or the Memorial University of Newfoundland or various record offices, including a small number for ships from Northern Ireland at PRONI.

Further reading

K. Smith, C. and M. Watts, *Records of Merchant Shipping and Seamen* (PRO, 1998)

C. and M. Watts, *My Ancestor was a Merchant Seaman* (Society of Genealogists, 1986)

There is also a useful series of PRO leaflets on records of merchant seamen and shipping.

Emigration

Many millions of Irish people left Ireland to seek their fortunes elsewhere. The United States was the most popular destination, while large numbers went to Canada, Australia and Britain. Unfortunately there are very few official records of their departure, and in most cases the authorities in the countries where they settled are likely to have better records of their arrival. A few lists for ships leaving ports in Northern Ireland, and related records, can be found at the Public Record Office of Northern Ireland (PRONI).

The few relevant emigration records at the PRO include a register of emigrants to North America between 1773 and 1776 (T 47). Irish men and women were also among those transported to Australia between 1788 and 1867. Details appear in the convict transportation registers in series HO 11, which provide the name of the ship on which the convict sailed, as well as the date and place of conviction and the term of the sentence. A database of people sent from Ireland can be found on the website of the National Archives of Ireland (http://www.nationalarchives.ie).

Outwards passenger lists between 1890 and 1960 include details of passengers leaving Britain by sea for destinations outside Europe and the Mediterranean. Many ships called at Queenstown (now Cobh) near Cork, before making the Atlantic crossing to the United States and Canada. The passenger lists for these ships give the name, age, occupation and previous address of passengers. They are arranged by year and port, and can be found in BT 27. Unfortunately, some lists are missing.

ⓘ **Remember**

There are huge numbers of passenger lists in BT 27. You therefore need to know approximately when and where a person left and the ship he or she went on.

It may be possible to find details of the emigration of individuals – or, much more probably, groups of emigrants – in the Colonial Office's correspondence with various colonies and in Foreign Office correspondence with British representatives abroad.

There is at present no comprehensive introduction to emigration records, although the PRO will publish Roger Kershaw's guide to the subject in early 2002. There is, however, a good section on the subject in A. Bevan, *Tracing Your Ancestors in the Public Record Office*.

Immigration

An increasing number of passenger lists for ships arriving in America are being published in books, on CD-ROM or on the internet. Many of these can be found at the library of the Society of Genealogists. Of particular interest is I. A. Glazier and M. Tepper, *The Famine Immigrants: Irish Immigrants arriving at the Port of New York, 1846–1851*, which contains 650,000 names. A useful website containing a number of lists is run by the American Immigrant Ship Transcription Guild (http://www.istg.rootsweb.com).

The following archives may be able to help locate ancestors who emigrated from Ireland:

▼ **National Archives of Canada**
   395 Wellington Street
   Ottawa
   Ontario K1A 0N3
   Canada
   Internet: http://www.archives.ca

▶ National Archives and Records Administration
700 Pennsylvania Avenue, NW
Washington, DC 20408
USA
Internet: http://www.nara.gov

▶ National Archives of New Zealand
10 Mulgrave Street
Thorndon
Wellington
New Zealand
Internet: http://www.archives.govt.nz

▶ National Archives of Australia
Queen Victoria Terrace
Parkes ACT 2600
Australia
Internet: http://www.naa.gov.au

There are no passenger lists for arrivals in Britain, because Irish people were British subjects. For recent arrivals there are registrations of British citizenship declared by British subjects or citizens of the Irish Republic, between 1948 and 1969, in series HO 334. These records are arranged by registration number rather than by name, so are difficult to use. More detail is given in section 2.5 of R. Kershaw and M. Pearsall, *Immigrants and Aliens: A Guide to Sources on UK Immigration and Citizenship.*

Although it can be difficult to find out about the arrival of individuals on the mainland of Britain, it is possible to identify Irish people in the censuses between 1841 and 1891 (and the 1901 census will be available in 2002.) It is quite rare, however, to find either the town or county of birth.

During the 1840s and 1850s the arrival of large numbers of Irish people in Britain caused considerable problems. Many arrived destitute, and besieged workhouses seeking assistance. Residents and local Poor Law authorities sought the help of central government, and there are letters and petitions in the correspondence of the Poor Law Commissioners in MH 12. This series also includes letters from local medical officers of health, particularly for Liverpool, on the squalid conditions the migrants lived in. There were also anti-Irish and anti-Catholic disturbances. Correspondence about this unrest can be found in HO 45, HO 52 and HO 144.

Many Irish men were employed in building and maintaining the railways and canals. The PRO has records of the pre-nationalization railway and canal companies, although the survival of staff registers is somewhat patchy. In addition, some railway records are held by the National Railway Museum in York and the National Archives of Scotland in Edinburgh. A good introduction to these records is T. Richards, *Was Your Grandfather a Railwayman?* or Cliff Edwards' comprehensive *Railway Records* (PRO, 2001).

Among the oddest collections of records at the PRO of use to the family historian are the registers of habitual drunkards between 1903 and 1914 (MEPO 6) and habitual criminals between 1869 and 1940 (PCOM 2 and MEPO 6). These include Irish people and contain considerable amounts of information, including photographs, aliases and distinguishing marks.

Royal Irish Constabulary

Between 1836 and 1922 Ireland (outside Dublin) was policed by the Royal Irish Constabulary. The service records for the 85,000 men who served in the Constabulary are in HO 184.

These registers are arranged by service number, but there are separate alphabetical indexes. The registers normally give name, age, height, religion, county of birth, original trade, marital status, places served and date of retirement. HO 184 also includes separate registers for the Auxiliaries (better known as the 'Black and Tans') who were recruited, generally from ex-servicemen, to suppress unrest between 1919 and 1921. Records of pensions and allowances made to officers and their widows and children are in PMG 48. The PRO's leaflet *Records of the Royal Irish Constabulary* (Domestic Records Information 54) describes these records in more detail. It can be downloaded from the PRO's website.

Copies of the *Royal Irish Constabulary List* for various dates between 1881 and 1908 are at the Society of Genealogists, as are several lists of staff members. More about the Constabulary can be found in J. Herlihy, *The Royal Irish Constabulary*. There is also a website, with a searchable database, at http://www.esatclear.ie/~ric/.

Before 1836 there were a number of local police forces in Ireland. Some information about the careers of super-annuated constables can be found in volume 26 of the Parliamentary Papers for 1831–2, which is available on microfiche at the PRO.

Customs and Excise

Records relating to appointments to the Irish Revenue Police, 1830–57, are in CUST 111. This was a force formed to combat the distillation of illicit alcohol and controlled by the Board of Excise (from 1849, the Board of Inland Revenue). Other records relating to Irish excisemen between 1824 and 1833 are in CUST 110.

There are also some records for Irish customs officers. Pay lists and staff lists between 1684 and 1826 are in CUST 20. The pension records in CUST 39 cover the period between 1785 and 1851.

The Easter Rising (1916) and the War of Independence (1919–1921)

There are numerous records relating to these events, and many of them contain genealogical information. There are, for example, registers containing biographical information about prominent nationalist politicians and activists from the mid-1880s in CO 904, supplemented by later material in WO 35. There are reports about ambushes, protests and arson attacks as the rising spread through the country between 1918 and 1921. In addition, WO 35 contains lists of civilians prosecuted for supporting the rebels.

After the Irish Free State had been established in 1922, several commissions were established to compensate people for damage to property and personal injury between January 1919 and July 1921. The records are in CO 762, CO 905 and T 80. The PRO has a leaflet entitled *Records of the Easter Rising* (Overseas Records Information 11) and a source sheet *Ireland, 1920–1922* (Source Sheet 6). The leaflet can be downloaded from the PRO's website.

Minor sources

These records may also be of interest:

- Association oath roll of nobility and gentry of Ireland now in England.   C 213

- Contributors to and relief of English subjects in Ireland, 1642 (arranged by county, hundred and parish).   SP 28, E 179

- Irish pedigrees, compiled by Lord Burghley and Sir Joseph Williamson in the sixteenth and seventeenth centuries, and notes on Irish genealogy.   SP 63

- List of borrowers and subscribers, arranged by county and local association, for the Irish Reproductive Loan set up to relieve the poor during the famine of 1822 in Munster and Connaught, 1822–1874.   T 91

- Lists of subscribers and nominees to the Irish State Tontines, 1773, 1775 and 1777.   NDO 1, NDO 2, NDO 3

- Nominations for appointments to the Irish Coastguard, 1821–49.   ADM 175

- State Papers, Ireland (1509–1782), containing dispatches from Ireland to the government in London, including petitions for land, letters from individuals and requests for funds. These records have been largely indexed and published between 1509 and 1704.
       SP 60–SP 67

- Tenancy files of the Irish Sailors' and Soldiers' Trust, which provided 4,000 cottages for ex-servicemen in the North and South.   AP 7

Family Records Centre

The Family Records Centre in London has many records that may contain details of ancestors who crossed the Irish Sea.

The FRC is a service for family historians, set up in 1997 by the Office for National Statistics (ONS) and the Public Record Office. It provides a comprehensive reference resource, including indexes to the major sources for family history in the United Kingdom; microfilm copies of a wide range of documents, including the censuses for England and Wales; CD-ROMs and online search facilities; and a large collection of reference books, indexes and maps.

No original documents are kept at the FRC. You can see the originals of *some* categories of material (but not the census) at the PRO at Kew. For a guide to the FRC, see J. Cox, *Never Been Here Before?*

▼ **Family Records Centre**
  1 Myddelton Street
  London EC1R 1UW
  Telephone: 020 8392 5300
  Telephone for birth, marriage and death certificates:
  0151 471 4800
  Fax: 020 8392 5307
  Internet: http://www.pro.gov.uk/frc/

You can visit the FRC in person without an appointment. If you are disabled, ring first, as disabled parking spaces need to be booked in advance, on 020 7533 6436.

Opening times (closed Sundays and public holidays):

Monday	9 a.m. to 5 p.m.
Tuesday	10 a.m. to 7 p.m.
Wednesday	9 a.m. to 5 p.m.
Thursday	9 a.m. to 7 p.m.
Friday	9 a.m. to 5 p.m.
Saturday	9.30 a.m. to 5 p.m.

Birth, marriage and death records after 1 July 1837

The birth, marriage and death records held at the FRC are for England and Wales only; the indexes are on the ground floor. The Irish equivalents, up to 1922, are available in Dublin; after that, they split between Dublin and Belfast.

It is not easy to identify the Irish ancestry of people described in the birth, marriage and death certificates. Only after 1969 did parents of newborn children have to supply their own place of birth. Although the date and place of birth of the deceased appear on death certificates, you cannot identify Irish ancestry from the index – only from the certificate itself.

The system will be familiar to anyone who has ordered certificates at the General Register Office in Dublin. To obtain a certificate, you need to consult the registers to find the correct reference. The document can then either be collected a few days later or be posted to you. At the time of writing, the cost of each certificate is £6.50.

For more about English and Welsh certificates, see *Using Birth, Marriage and Death Records*.

Armed forces returns

Also on the ground floor of the FRC you will find various registers for the armed forces, including Army registers of births and marriages 1761–1965 and of deaths 1796–1965, both in the UK and abroad. From 1796, there are also the Army chaplains' returns of births, marriages and deaths for soldiers serving abroad. These records include men who served in Irish regiments. This series of registers also includes the Royal Navy from 1881 and the Royal Air Force from 1920. They are indexed, although you will have to have a rough idea of when an event occurred. In addition, there are indexes to men who died while serving in the forces during the two world wars and the Boer War.

Census

The census reveals that considerable numbers of Irish people lived in England and Wales. In 1871 there were 566,540 men and women born in Ireland who were resident in England. Fortunately it can be relatively easy to track these people down, especially if you know where they were living at about the time of the census, which was normally taken in April. The earliest census for which records have been kept centrally is the 1841 census. The latest one available is for 1891. The 1901 census will be made available online on 2 January 2002.

Census records can be consulted on the first floor at the FRC. English and Welsh census returns are very similar to their Irish counterparts and contain much the same information – that is, name, age, marital status, relationship to head of household, occupation, and place of birth. All censuses thus identify individuals born in Ireland. However, it is unusual for the exact town or county to be given, which can be frustrating. Even more than other migrants to Britain, the Irish tended to form close-knit communities, often in the poorest districts of a town, so it is not uncommon to find whole streets full of people born in Ireland. Because of the time when the census was taken – spring – one can often find gangs of Irish seasonal workers: men and women who came across to work on market gardens and farms.

Census records are arranged by enumeration districts within registration districts or sub-districts (i.e. they are arranged by place rather than name). Surname indexes, where they exist, can help you to track down an individual. There are name indexes for the whole of the 1881 census, most of that for 1851, and parts of the other censuses. The 1881 census index is on CD-ROM and is available at libraries around the country and at the FRC. When the 1901 census is released online in January 2002, it will be searchable by surname, address, place and institution. In addition, there are a number of street indexes to London and large towns and cities, which can make searching considerably easier if you know the name of the street where an ancestor lived at about the time of the census. For more about census records, see *Using Census Records*.

Nonconformist registers

Also available at the FRC are the nonconformist records. By the time of the introduction of national registration of births, marriages and deaths in 1837, perhaps a quarter of the population did not belong to the Church of England. The law said that, to have legal status, baptisms, marriages and burials had to be performed in Anglican churches, although by the end of the eighteenth century this was widely ignored.

Nonconformists (also called dissenters) preferred their own Baptist, Congregational or, above all, Methodist chapels. With the introduction of national registration, nonconformist chapels were asked to send their registers to the government, and these records were eventually transferred to the PRO.

The nonconformist registers have been indexed and the information added to the *International Genealogical Index (IGI)*, an index to millions of baptisms, marriages and burials compiled from church registers and covering approximately 1538–1885. It can also be accessed on the internet at http://www.familysearch.org, and has been supplemented by the *Vital Records Index – British Isles*. Both are published by the LDS Church.

Microfiche copies of the *IGI* can be seen at the FRC and the PRO. Both the SoG and the LDS Church have copies, too.

There are very few Catholic registers amongst this material. However, a number of registers for Catholic parishes in England have been transcribed and can be found at the Society of Genealogists.

For further information about these registers, see *Using Birth, Marriage and Death Records*.

Wills

Before 1858, in the English system wills could be proved in a number of different places. The most important of these courts, because it covered the whole of England and Wales, was the Prerogative Court of Canterbury (PCC). Wealthy Irish merchants based in London, or even in Ireland itself or the colonies, might have their wills proved in the PCC. Nor was it only the wealthy who used this court, for it was not uncommon for soldiers and sailors to have their wills proved there.

Most PCC wills have been indexed, and these indexes are available at the FRC, the PRO and the SoG. Copies of PCC wills are also available at the PRO and the FRC. The SoG has various listings of Irish wills proved in the PCC.

These wills can be tricky to use. The staff at the FRC and PRO can help you, and there are a number of pamphlets available explaining the intricacies of the system, including the PRO's Pocket Guide *Using Wills*.

Other useful resources in England

Society of Genealogists (SoG)

The library at the Society of Genealogists contains a large collection of records and finding aids, some of which are unique. The library covers Scottish and Northern Irish records, as well as English and Welsh.

You do not have to be a member of the Society of Genealogists to use its library, although you do have to pay a fee. You can visit it without an appointment. It is conveniently located for you to combine a trip there with a trip to the FRC.

▼ **Society of Genealogists**
 14 Charthouse Buildings
 Goswell Road
 London EC1M 7BA
 Telephone: 020 7251 8799
 Internet: http://www.sog.org.uk/

Opening times (closed Sundays and Mondays):

Tuesday	10 a.m. to 6 p.m.
Wednesday	10 a.m. to 8 p.m.
Thursday	10 a.m. to 8 p.m.
Friday	10 a.m. to 6 p.m.
Saturday	10 a.m. to 6 p.m.

Family History Centres

These centres, set up by the Church of Jesus Christ of Latter-day Saints (commonly known as Mormons), give access to a number of indexes and records useful to family historians. To find out if there is one near you, contact:

▼ **The Genealogical Society of Utah**
   British Isles Family History Service Centre
   185 Penns Lane
   Sutton Coldfield
   West Midlands B76 8JU

Alternatively, you will find addresses for the centres on the Latter-day Saints website (http://www.LDS.org.uk) or in Pauline Saul, *The Family Historian Enquiries Within* (FFHS, 1995).

RESEARCHING IRISH ANCESTORS IN IRELAND

Most of your research into your Irish ancestors will naturally have to be undertaken in Ireland. However, there are an increasing number of websites, books and CD-ROMs that can help you before you arrive. For more about these, see Further Reading on p. 54.

The Irish administrative tradition is similar to that of England, which means that most of the records are like the ones used in researching English ancestry. In particular, birth, marriage and death certificates, and census returns, are virtually identical. Apart from a few early legal documents and some Catholic parish registers, which may be in Latin, the records are likely to be in English.

Much of your research can be done in Dublin, although you might need to visit Belfast, too, if your ancestors came from Northern Ireland. In addition, most counties, north as well as south, have one or more family history and heritage centre where you can find local material.

The places you are most likely to need to visit are given below.

In Dublin

▼ **National Archives of Ireland**
  Bishops Street
  Dublin 8
  Telephone: 01 407 2300
  Internet: http://www.nationalarchives.ie

The National Archives is the Irish Republic's equivalent of the Public Record Office, and also holds pre-1922 material on Northern Ireland. As mentioned earlier, many of its records were destroyed by fire in 1922.

▼ National Library of Ireland
Kildare Street
Dublin 2
Telephone: 01 603 0200
Internet: http://www.nli.ie

The National Library is Ireland's equivalent of the British Library. The Library is also home to the Chief Herald of Ireland, and the Genealogical Office.

▼ General Register Office
8–11 Lombard Street East
Dublin 2
Telephone: 01 635 4000
Internet: http://www.groireland.ie

The GRO holds birth, marriage and death records for Ireland between 1864 and 1921, and for the Republic from 1922 to the present day.

ⓘ Remember
To ring Dublin from outside the Republic, you have to add the international prefix 00 353 and omit the initial 0 in the dialling code. Thus, to ring the National Archives from Britain, you need to dial 00 353 1407 2300.

▼ Dublin City Archives
City Assembly House
58 South William Street
Dublin 2
Telephone: 01 677 5877

The City Archives holds the historic records of the municipal government of Dublin, from medieval times to the present. Of particular interest are records of freemen from 1468.

▼ Representative Church Body Library
Braemor Park
Rathgar
Dublin 14
Telephone: 01 492 3979
Internet: http://www.ireland.anglican.org/library

Holds many records relating to the Anglican Church of Ireland.

In Belfast

▼ Public Record Office of Northern Ireland
66 Balmoral Avenue
Belfast BT9 6NY
Telephone: 028 9025 5905
Internet: http://www.proni.nics.gov.uk

The Public Record Office of Northern Ireland (PRONI) is the major archive in the North. As well as official records of the Northern Ireland government, it has considerable holdings of personal and business papers going back to before partition. For its holdings of passenger lists, see p. 26.

▶ General Register Office of Northern Ireland
Oxford House
49–55 Chichester Street
Belfast BT1 4HL
Telephone: 028 9025 2021
Internet: http://www.nisra.gov.uk

The GRO for Northern Ireland holds birth, marriage and death certificates for Northern Ireland. Its holdings are explained in a leaflet, *Records and Search Services*, which can be downloaded from its website or sent by post.

▶ Ulster Historical Foundation
12 College Street East
Belfast BT1 5DD
Telephone: 028 9033 2288
Internet: http://www.uhf.org.uk

The Foundation organizes conferences, provides research services, and publishes books on aspects of Ulster and Irish genealogy.

ⓘ Remember
Even if you're planning to do a great deal of on-the-spot research, you may be able to save time and effort by making use of relevant websites, books and CD-ROMs.

Civil registration

The Irish system of civil registration of births, marriages and
deaths formally began on 1 January 1864. However, between
1 April 1845 and 31 December 1863 non-Roman Catholics
had to register their marriages with the authorities. These
records are held at the General Register Offices in Dublin and
Belfast, and are divided thus:

	Dublin	**Belfast**
Birth certificates	1864–1922 all Ireland; 1922	1864 to present Northern Ireland only to present Republic
Marriage certificates	1864 to present Republic	1922 to present Northern Ireland only
Death certificates	1864–1922 all Ireland; 1922 to present Republic	1864 to present Northern Ireland only; indexes available only from 1922

In Northern Ireland, marriage certificates between 1845 and
1921 are still with local registrars.

The system of getting access to the certificates is very similar to
that at the Family Records Centre in London. There are four
registers per year, and you need to note down details from the
register before you can order certificates. In Dublin, a fee is
charged to search the registers (currently IR £12 per day);
individual certificates cost IR £5.50 at present. In Belfast,
certificates currently cost £7, and no fee is charged for
searching the registers. The LDS Church Family History
Centres have microfilm copies for some indexes.

In addition, the GROs have registers relating to maritime, consular and military births, marriages and deaths (see pp. 17 and 23).

The information given on certificates is very similar to that on their English equivalents. For more details, see pp. 24–5 of the PRO Pocket Guide *Using Birth, Marriage and Death Records*.

Census

Censuses have been held in Ireland every ten years since 1821. Unfortunately, few records survive before 1901, the majority having either been pulped as waste paper during the First World War or destroyed during the Four Courts fire in 1922. The surviving records are either at PRONI (for Northern Ireland) or the National Archives (for the rest of Ireland). Abstracts from the 1841 and 1851 censuses are also available on a CD-ROM, *Irish Source Records*, published by Broderbund.

Unlike in mainland Britain, the 1901 and 1911 census returns for the whole of Ireland are readily available for inspection at the National Archives. No census returns for these dates are yet at PRONI. Local heritage centres may also have copies for their counties.

The information these records contain is very similar to that found on their English and Scottish equivalents, although in 1901 and 1911 householders were also asked to state length of marriage, and whether individuals could read and write or speak Irish. Provided you know an address, they are quite easy to use.

Parish registers

Roman Catholic

As the Roman Catholic faith was illegal until 1778 and then merely tolerated until 1829, there are few Catholic parish registers before the 1820s. They are almost entirely for baptisms and marriages, though death or burial entries occur occasionally. Baptism entries do, however, include the names of sponsors and witnesses.

Most parish registers before 1880 have been microfilmed by the National Library of Ireland. After this date, they are often with the parish priest. The microfilm copies of the registers can be consulted at the Library, and PRONI has copies relating to the six counties and border areas in the Republic.

Church of Ireland

In 1560 the Anglican Church of Ireland became the established church in Ireland. Unlike its sister church in England, it never had the support of the majority of the population. Its congregations were largely made up of English migrants and members of the Anglo-Irish communities, although nonconformists and Catholics often legitimized marriages and baptisms in the church. The majority of registers begin during the eighteenth century. In 1876 most registers were deposited at the Four Courts, where they were destroyed in 1922. Surviving registers may be with the parish; at the National Archives; at PRONI (for Northern Ireland); or with the Representative Church Body Library. Noel Reid (ed.), *A Table of Church of Ireland Parochial Records and Copies* lists which records are held where.

Nonconformist

Various nonconformist (or dissenting) sects, including the Quakers, Presbyterians and Congregationalists, established themselves in Ireland (particularly in the North) during the seventeenth and eighteenth centuries. As the authorities looked on them suspiciously, their parish registers usually do not begin much before the 1840s. Surviving records are kept by the churches themselves, or at PRONI.

ⓘ Remember

The Society of Genealogists Library has copies of some Irish census records. It also has copies of many Roman Catholic, Church of Ireland and nonconformist parish registers.

Wills and testaments

The system of administration of probate in Ireland was very similar to that in England. It should, however, be remembered that until well into the nineteenth century the vast majority of people were too poor to leave a will, so the records discussed below are largely for the Anglo-Irish landowners and merchants in the larger towns.

Before 1858, wills were proved in a court of the Church of Ireland. The most important of these was the Prerogative Court of Armagh, which – despite its name – met in Dublin. Each diocese also had its own consistory court for dealing with less important wills.

In 1858 a national and secular probate register was established in Dublin, along English lines, to administer wills. Eleven district registries were also set up. Much of the pre-1857 material, as well as wills proved under the new system to 1900, were lost in the Four Courts fire. However, some indexes survive, and these can contain useful genealogical information. Indexes to many Irish wills between 1536 and 1857 can be found in the *Irish Source Records* CD-ROM.

The National Archives has surviving records up to 1922, as well as wills proved between 1922 and 1981 for the Irish Republic. PRONI has records of the district registries for Belfast and Londonderry (1900–86) and Armagh (1900–21 only). Copies of a number of these indexes can be found in the SoG Library.

ⓘ **Remember**

A number of people, particularly those with financial interests in England, preferred to have wills proved in the Prerogative Court of Canterbury (see p. 37).

OTHER SOURCES FOR IRISH ANCESTORS

Newspapers

The first Irish newspapers date from the eighteenth century, and contain much the same information as their English counterparts. Initially they were only published in Dublin, but they gradually spread across Ireland.

Copies of most Irish newspapers are held by the National Library in Dublin. The British Library Newspaper Library, Colindale, London NW9 5HE (Telephone: 020 8412 7353; internet: http://www.bl.uk/collections/newspaper) also has many Irish newspapers.

Directories

The first trade and street directories were published for Dublin in 1751. Over the next hundred years or so, coverage slowly spread through the rest of the island. The most important of these directories was Thom's, which also included details of official appointments. Other important directories were Pigot's, Slater's and Wilson's. The PRO library has a run of Thom's between 1844 and 1928. The SoG also has a number of directories, the earliest dating from 1761. In Dublin, both the National Archives and the National Library have runs of various directories, while in Belfast copies of directories, particularly for the six counties, are at PRONI.

School and university registers

Until 1849 the only university in Ireland was Trinity College
Dublin. In 1849 Queen's Colleges were founded in Belfast, Cork
and Galway. In 1880 they were merged with a new foundation
in Dublin to form the Royal (later National) University of
Ireland. The PRO library has calendars for the National
University of Ireland, Dublin, which list students and lecturers.
The Society of Genealogists has similar, if incomplete, runs.

The SoG also has a small collection of histories and published
registers of pupils for a number of schools, particularly public
schools, in Ireland. Both the National Archives and PRONI
have collections of records of national (state) schools from the
1830s, including many registers. The National Archives
website (http://www.nationalarchives.ie) contains a searchable database of these records.

Maps

The first detailed maps of Ireland were drawn up during the
1830s and early 1840s to show land ownership and facilitate
the introduction of a new land tax. Townland maps, on a scale
of 6 inches to 1 mile were completed for the whole country by
1842. This massive undertaking ensured that the island was
surveyed with a degree of thoroughness and accuracy unique
for its time. The completed maps show Ireland as it was just
before the ravages of the Famine. Papers relating to these
maps are in the National Archives in Dublin, and copies of
the maps are at the PRO (in ZOS 7).

The PRO has large numbers of other maps of Ireland. These
begin with Gough's Map of 1576, and include a set of 1-inch

Ordnance Survey maps published in 1851 and 1852 (ZOS 14). There are catalogues and card indexes to help users find what they want. There is also a useful free leaflet explaining the PRO's map collections and how they are arranged: *Maps in the PRO* (Domestic Records Leaflet 72). This can be downloaded from the PRO's website or requested from the helpline (telephone: 020 8392 5200).

The largest collection of maps in Ireland is at the National Library. A searchable index to this material can be found on its website (http://www.nli.ie). PRONI has many maps for Northern Ireland.

Records on aspects of property

There are various records connected to land-owning or property-owning that can be used to flesh out other sources. It should, however, be remembered that these usually exclude the mass of the population, who were either landless labourers or small tenant farmers.

Griffith's Valuation

The Primary Valuation of Ireland, popularly known as Griffith's Valuation, was a survey of land and property carried out between 1846 and 1865 by Sir Richard Griffith. Its purpose was to establish a means by which a tax could be calculated for the upkeep of the poor. The survey lists names of landowners and tenants, together with the extent and value of their property. About 1.25 million people appear in these records, which means that the valuation can to some extent be used as a replacement for the missing census records – although only the name of the landowner or tenant is given. The valuation was published, and copies are available at the National Archives and PRONI (for Northern Ireland). There are also indexes at the Society of Genealogists. The indexes may also help you identify the place where a person was born, which will help you track down parish registers.

In the Irish Republic, valuations of property from 1846 have been administered by the Valuation Office of Ireland. Its records are open to inspection, on payment of a fee. For individual properties, these registers will tell you the occupier's name, acreage of the property, and its rateable value. The address is:

▼ **Valuation Office of Ireland**
   Irish Life Centre
   Abbey Street Lower
   Dublin 1
   Telephone: 01 817 1000
   Internet: http://www.valoff.ie

The equivalent records for Northern Ireland are at PRONI.

Tithe applotment books

Between 1823 and 1838, tithe applotment books were compiled to determine the level of tithes to be paid to the Church of Ireland. This survey identified all landowners and the amount of land they owned, together with the crops they grew and the quality of the land they farmed. The books, however, are by no means complete, as some parishes were too poor for tithes to be levied. These records are to be found at the National Archives, with copies for Northern Ireland at PRONI. They have been published both on microfiche and on CD-ROMs.

The 1873 return of owners of land

Between 1873 and 1876 a survey of land ownership, nick-named the New Domesday, was conducted throughout Britain and Ireland. The returns are arranged by county, and list the landowner together with the extent and valuation of his or her land. They were published as a Parliamentary paper. Copies are at the PRO, the National Archives and PRONI.

Flax growers' bounty list

During the eighteenth century Ireland, and Ulster in partic-ular, established a reputation as a producer of fine linen made from flax. At various times the government introduced special incentives to encourage the production of linen, often giving away spinning wheels and looms. In 1796 the Irish Linen Board published a list, now in the National Archives, of almost 60,000 individuals who had awards for planting an acre or more of flax.

FURTHER READING AND OTHER RESOURCES

There are numerous books and websites helping people trace their Irish ancestry. Some of the most useful are given below, plus a list of heritage centres in Ireland, many of which have websites. The majority of them belong to the Irish Family History Foundation, and some of them offer commissioned research services.

Books

A. Bevan, *Tracing Your Ancestors in the Public Record Office* (5th edn, PRO, 1999)

A. J. Camp, *Sources for Irish Genealogy in the Library of the Society of Genealogists* (Society of Genealogists, 1998)

J. Cox, *Never Been Here Before?* (PRO, 1998)

B. Davis, *Irish Family History Research* (FFHS, 1997)

B. Davis, *An Introduction to Irish Research* (FFHS, 1998)

R. F. Foster, *Modern Ireland 1600–1972* (Penguin, 1988)

S. Fowler and W. Spencer, *Army Service Records for Family Historians* (PRO, 1998)

I. A. Glazier and M. Tepper, *The Famine Immigrants: Irish Immigrants arriving at the Port of New York, 1846–1851* (Genealogical Publishing Company, Baltimore, 1983–96)

I. A. Glazier, *The Famine Immigrants: Lists of Irish Immigration to the Port of New York, 1846–1857* (Genealogical Publishing Company, Baltimore, 1983)

J. Grenham, *Tracing Your Irish Ancestors* (2nd edn, Gill and Macmillan, 1999)

S. Helferty, *Directory of Irish Archives* (3rd edn, Irish Academic Press, 2000)

J. Herlihy, *The Royal Irish Constabulary* (Four Courts Press, 1997)

R. Kershaw and M. Pearsall, *Immigrants and Aliens: A Guide to Sources on UK Immigration and Citizenship* (PRO, 2000)

I. Maxwell, *Tracing your Ancestors in Northern Ireland* (Stationery Office, 1997)

T. McCarthy, *The Irish Roots Guide* (Lilliput, 1991)

B. Mitchell, *A Guide to Irish Churches and Graveyards* (Genealogical Publishing Company, Baltimore, 1990)

R. K. O'Neill, *Ulster Libraries, Archives, Museums and Ancestral Heritage Centres* (Ulster Historical Foundation, 1997)

E. M. Ódúill and S. C. Ffeary-Smyrl, *Irish Civil Registration: Where do I Start?* (Council of Irish Genealogical Organizations, 2000)

A. Prochaska, *Irish History from 1700: A Guide to Sources in the Public Record Office* (British Records Association, 1986)

J. Reakes, *Help! My Ancestor is Irish and I'm Stuck* (Immigration and Family History Centre, Queensland, 1997)

N. Reid (ed.), *A Table of Church of Ireland Parochial Records and Copies* (Irish Family History Society, 1994)

N. Reid, *Directory of Parish Registers Indexed in Ireland* (Irish Family History Society, 1997)

T. Richards, *Was Your Grandfather a Railwayman?* (3rd edn, FFHS, 1995)

J. P. Ryan, *Irish Church Records: Their History, Availability and Use in Family and Local History Research* (Flyover Press, 1992)

The PRO publishes a useful series of Pocket Guides on family history. See especially *Using Army Records; Using Birth, Marriage and Death Certificates; Using Census Records;* and *Using Wills* (all published in 2000).

The magazine *Irish Roots* specializes in Irish genealogy. In addition, *Ancestors* (published by the Public Record Office), *Family History Monthly*, *Family Tree Magazine* and *Practical Family History* regularly carry articles about Ireland. These magazines are sold at the PRO, FRC, SoG and at major newsagents.

A number of Irish records and their indexes have been copied and appear on an increasing number of CD-ROMs. These can usually be bought either singly or as part of a software package such as *Generations* or *Family Tree Maker*. They can be purchased at the SoG or from suppliers who advertise in the magazines listed above.

The following are available on CD-ROMs published by Broderbund: some local trade directories, the index to Griffith's Valuation, tithe applotment books for Northern Ireland, and the 1796 list of awards for flax growing.

Websites

It is increasingly easy to conduct genealogical research over the internet. There are tens of thousands of genealogical websites of varying degrees of accuracy and usefulness. The websites for the institutions holding genealogical material are listed in the main body of the text above. There are a number of other sites that may be useful for your research, including:

http://www.cyndislist.com	Cyndi's List has links to over 60,000 genealogical sites around the world.
http://www.genuki.org.uk	The genealogical website for the United Kingdom and Ireland.
http://www.ireland.com/ancestors	Takes you to the genealogical pages of the *Irish Times*.
http://www.mayo-ireland.ie/general	The Irish Family History Foundation provides links to local research centres in Ireland.
http://homepage.eircom.net/~ifhs	The website of the Irish Family History Society.
http://www.local.ie/genealogy	The Local Ireland genealogy pages.
http://www.ancestryireland.com	The website of the Ulster Historical Foundation

Heritage Centres in Ireland

(telephone numbers are from outside Ireland)

▸ **Armagh Ancestry**
 42 English Street
 Armagh BT60 7BA
 Northern Ireland
 Tel: 028 3752 1802/8329
 Fax: 028 3751 0033

▸ **Brú Boru Heritage Centre**
 Cashel
 Co. Tipperary
 Republic of Ireland
 Tel: 00 353 62 61122
 Fax: 00 353 62 62700

▸ **Carlow Genealogy Project**
 Old School
 College Street
 Carlow
 Republic of Ireland
 Tel: 00 353 503 30850
 Fax: 00 353 503 30850

▸ **Cavan Heritage and Genealogy Centre**
 Cana House
 Farnham Street
 Cavan
 Co. Cavan
 Republic of Ireland
 Tel: 00 353 49 4361094
 Fax: 00 353 49 4331494

▸ **Clare Genealogy Centre**
 Corofin
 Co. Clare
 Republic of Ireland
 Tel: 00 353 65 6837955
 Fax: 00 353 65 6837540

▼Cork City Ancestral Project
c/o Cork County Library
Farranlea Road
Cork
Republic of Ireland
Tel: 00 353 21 54699

▼Donegal Ancestry Heritage Centre
Back Lane
Ramelton
Co. Donegal
Republic of Ireland
Tel: 00 353 74 51266
Fax: 00 353 74 51266

▼Dublin Heritage Group
2nd Floor
Cumberland House
Fenian Street
Dublin 2
Republic of Ireland
Tel: 00 353 1 459 1048/676 1628

▼Dún Laoghaire Rathdown Heritage Society
Moran Park House
Dún Laoghaire
Co. Dublin
Republic of Ireland
Tel: 00 353 1 280 6961, ext. 238
Fax: 00 353 1 280 6969

▼Dún na Sí Heritage Centre
Knockdanney
Moate
Co. Westmeath
Republic of Ireland
Tel: 00 353 902 81183
Fax: 00 353 902 81661

East Galway Family History Society
Woodford Heritage Centre
Main Street
Woodford
Co. Galway
Republic of Ireland
Tel: 00 353 509 49309
Fax: 00 353 509 49546

Fingal Heritage Project
The Carnegie Library
North Street
Swords
Co. Dublin
Republic of Ireland
Tel: 00 353 1 840 3629

Galway Family History Society West
Research Unit
Venture Centre
Liosbaun Estate
Tuam Road
Galway
Republic of Ireland
Tel: 00 353 91 756737

Heritage World
The Heritage Centre
26 Market Square
Dungannon
Co. Tyrone BT70 1AB
Northern Ireland
Tel: 028 872 4187
Fax: 028 875 2141

▶Irish Midlands Ancestry
Bury Quay
Tullamore
Co. Offaly
Republic of Ireland
Tel: 00 353 506 21421
Fax: 00 353 506 21421

▶Kildare Heritage & Genealogical Society
c/o Kildare County Library
Newbridge
Co. Kildare
Republic of Ireland
Tel: 00 353 45 433602

▶Kilkenny Ancestry
Rothe House
16 Parliament Street
Kilkenny City
Co. Kilkenny
Republic of Ireland
Tel: 00 353 56 22893
Fax: 00 353 56 22893

▶Killarney Genealogical Centre
Bishop's House
Killarney
Co. Kerry
Republic of Ireland
Tel: 00 353 64 35946

▶Leitrim Heritage Centre
c/o Leitrim County Library
Ballinamore
Co. Leitrim
Republic of Ireland
Tel: 00 353 78 44012
Fax: 00 353 78 44425

▼Limerick Archives
The Granary
Michael Street
Limerick
Republic of Ireland
Tel: 00 353 61 415125/312988
Fax: 00 353 61 312985

▼Longford Genealogical Centre
1 Church Street
Longford
Republic of Ireland
Tel: 00 353 43 41235

▼Mallow Heritage Centre
27–28 Bank Place
Mallow
Co. Cork
Republic of Ireland
Tel: 00 353 22 21778

▼Mayo North Family History Research Centre
Enniscoe
Castlehill
Ballina
Co. Mayo
Republic of Ireland
Tel: 00 353 96 31809
Fax: 00 353 96 31885

▼Mayo South Family Research Centre
Main Street
Ballinrobe
Co. Mayo
Republic of Ireland
Tel: 00 353 92 41214
Fax: 00 353 92 41214

Meath Heritage Centre
Trim
Co. Meath
Republic of Ireland
Tel: 00 353 46 36633
Fax: 00 353 46 37502

Monaghan Ancestral Research
Monaghan County Council
Cootehill Road
Monaghan
Republic of Ireland
Tel: 00 353 47 82304

Roscommon Heritage and Genealogy Centre
Strokestown
Co. Roscommon
Republic of Ireland
Tel: 00 353 78 33380

Sligo Heritage and Genealogy Centre
Aras Reddan
Temple Street
Sligo City
Co. Sligo
Republic of Ireland
Tel: 00 353 71 43728

Tipperary Heritage Unit
Family History Research Centre
Marian Hall
St. Michael's Street
Tipperary Town
Republic of Ireland
Tel: 00 353 62 52725
Fax: 00 353 62 52981

▼ Tipperary North Family History Foundation
The Gate House
Nenagh
Co. Tipperary
Republic of Ireland
Tel: 00 353 67 33850
Fax: 00 353 67 33586

▼ Waterford Heritage Ltd
Jenkin's Lane
Waterford
Republic of Ireland
Tel: 00 353 51 876123
Fax: 00 353 51 850645

▼ Wexford Genealogy Centre
Yola Farmstead
Tagoat
Co. Wexford
Republic of Ireland
Tel: 00 353 53 31177
Fax: 00 353 53 31177

▼ Wicklow Heritage Centre
Wicklow's Historic Gaol
Wicklow Town,
Co. Wicklow
Republic of Ireland
Tel: 00 353 404 20126
Fax: 00 353 404 61612

▼ Ulster Historical Foundation
12 College Square East
Belfast BT1 6DD
Northern Ireland
Tel: 028 9033 2288
Fax: 028 9023 9885